SHE

SHE

by

Bridget Callaghan

DREAMER
PUBLICATIONS

Publisher's Cataloging-In-Publication Data
(Prepared by The Donohue Group, Inc.)

Callaghan, Bridget.
  She / by Bridget Callaghan.
    pages ; cm
  Issued also as an ebook.
  ISBN: 978-1-937100-10-0
  1. Callaghan, Bridget. 2. Girls--Conduct of life--Anecdotes. 3. Self-actualization (Psychology) in children--Anecdotes. I. Title.
HQ783 .C35 2014
303.32/02   2014952519

PRINTED IN THE UNITED STATES OF AMERICA

For Riley

CONTENTS

Hitchhiking

The Brat: Part I

Scar

Christmas 1976

Lost

The Salad Bowl

Touching the Afro

The Dogs: Part I

The Brat: Part II

Confraternity

Better Cheddar

Pot

The Brat: Part III

Smoking

Special Events

The Dogs: Part II

The Brat: The End

Floater

HITCHHIKING

To her, a friend might be anyone outside. Most times She folded into a group of kids doing something like chasing a snake or playing on the rope swing in the back woods. Nobody was invited. One just showed up and showed interest.

She was with an older girl in the neighborhood. A girl who lived across the street and up the hill a little. The girl had sandy-blond hair that was always disheveled and covered the majority of her eyes. She noticed the girl would perpetually look down, as if reading an invisible book. Maybe the muscles in the back of her neck were weak. These idiosyncrasies mattered not, the girl was outside, and She wanted to play.

"What do you want to do?" She said.

"I'm going to hitchhike," the girl said and started walking.

She followed, thinking this might be fun.

They had rounded the corner, going outside of the double cul-de-sac—outside of their neighborhood— and onto an adjoining street. The girl stopped and looked up and down the road, and She did the same. Empty.

She watched as the girl planted her right foot on the street, raised her right arm, and said, "This is how you do it."

She watched as the girl's hand poked out of the knitted sweater, thumb up in the air. Like Fonzie's favorite gesture on *Happy Days*, but different.

She mimicked the stance and position, but the girl critiqued her performance. Under her new friend's tutelage, She was able to get it right. They stood there for a minute. Nothing.

Both agreed to play in the ditch until someone came by. She and the girl began to dig into the sand and gravel to make mud pies. They'd formed two very impressive chocolate and mulberry mud pies when the first car came along.

"Quick, get up," the girl said over her shoulder, already hurrying to the road.

She sprung up, wiped the sand off her pants, and climbed out of the ditch. The girl posed like before, and She was in tow, so proud, with her arm jutted out and raised high into the air—like the Statue of Liberty, but with much more exuberance. The car began to slow down, and She felt her stomach drop. Something wasn't right. The car was a silver-blue Cadillac, and the sun sparkled off the chrome around the headlights.

The car stopped in front of them. Both girls were silent as the window came down. The woman inside the car began to yell at them. The woman, a stranger to her, slapped the dashboard and screeched out words like *danger*, *bad*, and *mother*. The woman was right. Something was wrong, and now her mother was going to be involved, and holy hell was going to be paid. For what, She wasn't too sure.

She was four.

THE BRAT: PART I

The act of being a brat took a lot of energy. She would throw herself on the carpet when it was her turn to clear dishes. She used this obstinate act for too many years in her life. Maybe into later adolescence—ten, eleven years old. Imagine, rolling out of a high-back dining room chair and onto matted carpet, thrashing in agony because it's your turn to walk back and forth from the table to the kitchen. She writhed, yelled, and dug her heels into the carpet for extra effect.

To her, the worst part was her father's response: "Oh, the poor baby."

An early bratty moment came at Easter. The family was in Birmingham, enjoying the commemoration of the resurrection of the Lord. When it was time to pack up the station wagon, the matriarch and beloved grandmother, proposed a hunt for Easter treats. Every child had to find his or her treasure, and She watched as the older siblings each found a chocolate covered egg. Her imagination quickly started working. What was inside the eggs? More chocolate? Vanilla cream? Her thoughts went wild with visions of sweets. The eggs themselves were encased in cardboard and cellophane boxes. They were colored in soft pastels and lay on a bed of fake grass. The eggs reminded her of sleeping beauty. Delicate, lovely, and coveted by dwarfs.

The anticipation mounted. Turn by turn She searched for what was sure to be a chocolate ball of love and decadence.

Her love for chocolate was legendary, even at the age of two. She would scale the counters and cupboards in search of anything chocolate. If there was none, She'd suck on a piece of baker's chocolate that had been dipped in sugar. Like a junkie her heart rate escalated and palms perspired when She saw chocolate.

It was her turn to find her own egg. The insatiable sweet tooth that drove her every thought and action lit up like a disco ball. All eyes were on her. Under the table? No. In the cupboard? No. Someone took pity on her and moved the kitchen pantry door open to expose its content. There it was, staring at her—a pink bunny rabbit with glued-on eyes and a quirky, albeit happy, look on its face. She picked up the stuffed bunny and looked under its body. No chocolate egg. She looked to her family, puzzled. What was this stuffed bunny for?

"You like it?" her grandmother asked in a cheerful voice.

This was her chocolate egg? It took one second for her brain the register the fuzzy creature was not made of chocolate, nor was She going to get any chocolate. She was crushed, and the brat came out.

It started with a quivered lip and grew into a shaking scream of sorrow. She could hear the moans from the adults, trying to console her, but the levy had burst. She was not getting chocolate, but now She was painfully aware her reaction was disappointing. She was sent to the car. Such a brat.

Her bratty behavior evolved as She did. The consequences landed her in different forms hot water: grounding, ostracism by her siblings, knife threats, monkey bumps and noogies, abandonment at any public venue, and being told repeatedly how much She sucked. Probably because She did.

SCAR

One day when She was five, her brother rousted her from a warm bed. It was early Sunday morning, and their parents were still asleep. She, in many ways, was her sibling's plaything. She was too young to understand the difference between being female or male and yet, old enough to be coaxed into chasing a snake under the porch or to sit in the front of the toboggan sled because it was "fun" and a "great view."

This particular Sunday morning, her brother, the more elusive one, was playful and engaging. He was double her age and double her speed, height, and weight. After they made cinnamon toast and guzzled whole milk, her brother leaned over and tapped her on the shoulder. He said two of the most provocative words to be uttered: "You're it."

They darted around furniture and leapt up stairs and

around corners. She tried to keep up. She tried to catch him. If She could get him this one time, to be triumphant, to no longer be "it" would catapult her to the status of victor or contender, even if but for a moment.

She pursued her brother around the wicker chairs, and he made a dash for the kitchen. Aha! The kitchen included a rectangle counter top that jutted from the wall. Beyond that, there was no exit. Essentially, the kitchen was a dead end, and her brother would be trapped.

The speed and agility in his young legs allowed her brother to disappear beyond the counter. At full speed, her body electric with adrenalin, She rounded the corner. Her brain and mouth were ready to scream for the first time, "You're it! You're it! You're it!" She never expected her brother to be huddled by the lazy Susan, never expected him to pounce on her with a loud, "Boo."

Startled, She turned on her heels, away from her brother, and rammed her forehead into the counter's edge with a thud.

The scream She let out was as dramatic as the ribbons of blood that streamed down her nose and over her lips. It was the kind of scream that wakes parents up. Her mother and father reached her by the third wail. She was in between cries, hovering in that moment when all the air had been pressed out of her lungs, when her mother looked down upon her face, upon the silent mask of pain. Towels and wet napkins were placed over her head and face, as her mother tried to quiet her down.

The cries calmed to a purr of sniffles.

"It's turning purple," said her brother, providing color commentary as the injury progressed from a cut to a dent to a gash to . . . "Gross," he said.

Her father assessed the injury that puckered over her left eye. "It's gonna need stitches."

She stood like a scarecrow in the kitchen as her mother removed her bloodstained nightgown and dressed her in winter attire. Her father brushed the few inches of snow off the family station wagon, and her mother carried her down the porch stairs and gently placed her in the front seat of the car.

She sat silent as her father drove to the emergency room. She was silent for two reasons. First, She had never sat in the front seat of the family car. This position was saved for her mother or coveted by her older siblings. It was foreign land. The ashtray overflowed, the radio was within easy reach and plenty of room to swing her feet back and forth. Second, She was also painfully aware that She had never been alone with her father.

As they rounded the corner at Grandview Parkway, which ran along the shoreline, She stared at the fog of ice crystals that formed on the inside of the window. Then her father lit a cigarette, and her attention was drawn to him. He cracked the driver's window, and She watched the smoke twist in the air. Her father looked at her as She at him.

"Does it hurt?" he asked.

"No, not anymore."

CHRISTMAS 1976

For my beautiful siblings . . .

The heavy smell of incense woke her. The chime of the thurible chains sang as the priest went up and down the aisles of the packed church spreading ceremonial smoke on patrons. She enjoyed the thick smell because it reminded her of their grandparent's house. She wiped the sleep from her eyes, grabbed her Susie doll, and asked to be held by her father. Midnight Mass was almost over, and She didn't want to get lost in the exodus.

As the choir wailed "Joy to the World," everyone made their way outside. Her siblings were separated from their parents, and She kept her eye on them from her perch in her father's arms. The massive wooden exit doors were being held open by the ushers, and small cries and laments were heard as snow blew into the vestibule. A lot of snow. Driven by a lot of wind.

"Would you look at that?" her father said. "I'm going to have to shovel out the car."

While the parishioners had been singing their songs and inhaling the incense and witnessing the birthday of the Savior, Mother Nature had been dumping snow, commanding the north winds, and making a complete mess of the landscape. It took her father twenty minutes to get the car out of two feet of freshly fallen snow. It wasn't the fluffy, light snow that floats away with a mild breeze but the heavy, wet snowball-making kind of snow.

As the family made their way home, her father kept saying, "I hope we make it." He was referring to the hill that led to their house.

"I hope we make it." Again and again.

This statement piqued her anxiety. She didn't want to ask what would happen if they didn't make it. The 1972 Vista Cruiser banked left up East Timberlane Drive. The road started off flat, then gently sloped, and finally grew into an intimidating climb with an estimated 30 percent grade. When they hit the steeper part, the family could feel the tires begin to spin freely as her father pressed the accelerator. The car gently stopped at the middle hump of the incline. Her father put the car in reverse.

"I think we're going to end up in the ditch," her brother said.

She felt panic, as all her siblings did. Their father explained he could use speed and momentum to get them to the top of the hill. She believed him.

Again, the Vista Cruiser chugged to action and took on more speed as her father commandeered the automobile. She and her brothers and sister were sitting on the edge of the back seat. Each sibling rocked back and forth in unison, as if their weight and spirit could push their car in some magical way. Another five feet was all they traveled, still too far from home. Again, their father put the car in reverse and guided the automobile backward. This time, he miscalculated the road and backed the family cruiser into a snow bank.

"I was right," her brother shouted.

"Oh, shut it," their mother yelled. After some muffled swearing and heated discussion, it was determined that the family was indeed stuck.

Thank God She was wearing a dress and flimsy tights, because this qualified her to be carried through the cloud of thick snow. Again, her father scooped her out of the back seat, and they trudged home. The view from over her father's shoulder was surreal. She looked upon her siblings, who were hunched over like old ladies in the frozen food section of the grocery store. Each gust of wind pushed them about like tiny sailboats on the open ocean of white—nothing but white. It took only ten minutes to make the trek, but by the time the family had reached the foyer, all were covered in a layer of wet and mess.

They all quietly went to their rooms and got dressed for bed. She looked for Susie, her doll. Where was her doll? She began to panic. Had She left Susie at church? No! Worse! She had left Susie in the car. Out in the cold, dark car all alone.

"I left Susie out in the car!" She cried.

Her mother was reassuring and promised that Susie was not going to freeze and would, of course, forgive her.

She asked her father to go back and get her favorite doll, but he would have nothing to do with the request. She didn't like leaving anyone behind.

It was two in the morning by the time the house quieted down and all were in bed. Sleep overcame the frenzied feeling of anticipation. All day She had envisioned the den filled with stacks of presents, each child's stash lined up in tidy rows and their stockings fat with candy, tinker toys and, of course, toothbrushes. As sleep overtook her, the last conscious thought was of the doll, Susie, trying to find warmth within the confines of the Vista Cruiser.

* * *

Her sister was next to her bed telling her to get up. Though her eyes were fully opened, her sister appeared fuzzy. She sat up in bed and instantly pulled her blanket to her face.

"What's that smell?" She asked, but her sister was already exiting the bedroom. It seemed everyone in the house was up. She could see black smoke hugging the ceiling, which didn't make sense. She lumbered out of bed and toddled to the sitting room. There, all of her family members were standing together, forming a circle, and all were looking down at the floor.

As She approached her brother, he turned and announced, "Dad set the house on fire."

She looked at the place on the floor where everyone's eyes were transfixed. Where there should have been the family's brown leather chair, there was now a black circle of charred carpet and ash.

She was dazed and half asleep. One brother was staring out the picture window in the dining room. The window gave a lovely view of their very hilly front yard and the split roads of the neighborhood. The window was a perch, so to speak. She was curious as to what he was looking at and joined him at the window.

"I can hear the sirens," her brother said.

She heard them too. She pressed her nose against the glass and rested her lower lip on the sill. The tops of the trees were the first to catch the red and yellow lights of the massive fire truck. The tips of the branches pulsed with soft carnival-like light.

"I bet they get stuck on the hill too," her father said. "Or lost."

The lights grew more intense, and the ladder and nose of the fire truck poked from behind the corner of Timberlane Drive and Kaukauna Court, it's siren a deafening blare. The truck should have banked right to come to the rescue, but it kept going straight up the remainder of Timberlane Drive and past the Stewarts' house.

"Dumb bastards don't know where they're going," her father said, his hands on his hips, shaking his head. He looked more perturbed than worried about his scorched floor. "I told you they'd get lost."

She went back to the black mess, knelt down, and examined the floor more closely. It was then that She noticed a glob of milky-white plastic melted into the carpet. It had a face attached to it. Beanbag Bunny, who had been carelessly left under the leather chair, had been a victim of the fire. Its body no longer attached to the head, which was now one with the carpet pile. Beanbag Bunny was no more.

She looked at her mother and began to cry. First Susie's abandonment out in the Vista Cruiser and now the death of Beanbag Bunny. She couldn't hold back the tears anymore. Her mother told her to stop. The command was jarring. The tone suggested there were more important matters at hand than the loss of a stuffed animal. After a few more sobs, She grew quiet and made her way back to her siblings, back to the picture window.

"They'll find us," her sister said just as the fire truck, ablaze with color and sound, made a second pass by their house, back down Timberlane Drive, past the Vista Cruiser and Susie the doll.

LOST

She held the plastic bag like it was *the* prototype. So proud. Her father encouraged her puerile eagerness by saying, "You're so close to the ground, you'll fill up that bag with all the morels." Whatever morels were, She knew they grew in the woods and had the importance to capture her father's attention. She was determined to find all of them and capture his attention too.

"What do they look like?" She asked.

"They look like small sponges, you know, like a sponge." Her father made a motion as if cleaning a pot or the toilet. Something She'd never seen him do.

The coveted morel mushroom blossomed in early spring and tickled the explorer's and epicurean's mind. The fungus called out to the housebound, entrenched person who was paled by too much darkness and artificial light. "Walk in the woods," they said. "Get out. Find me. Eat me." It didn't matter if the event held as much promise as finding Sasquatch; it was fun and included a walk.

The family wasn't going to look in the back yard. That wasn't a challenge. They piled into the Chevy station wagon and drove thirty minutes out of town to a strip of interstate that abutted government land. Acres of overgrown woods with oaks, maples, ferns, and underbrush. She was told that morels grew close to stumps and the bottom of tree trunks, usually under leaves and vines. She made a mental note to look for logs and anything brown that may point the way to her treasure.

One by one, each family member exited the car and lined up. She was paired with her mother, of course. Her older siblings didn't want to be held back by her short legs and whining. Each pair chose a different direction into the wood, and off they went. Being early spring, the ground was cooler than the air, and She was forced to put on her winter coat. She and her mother made their way through sparse trees and thick underbrush. As they ventured further into the woods, the afternoon sunlight was filtered by the canopy into pointed shafts of gold.

The excitement of the trek wore off after a solid hour. She poked under stumps and spotted foliage with no success. And no success prevailed. Her feet began to hurt and so did her stomach. She decided that facing her siblings empty-handed was more attractive than starving to death. She encouraged her mother to abandon the search and head back to the car.

There was one problem. They had ventured too far into the woods, and her mother didn't trust an assessment of which way the car was. Both looked in every direction. There was no sign of a road or a worn path. And they could no longer hear the chatter of other family members.

"The car is that way," She said to her mother and pointed south. For her it wasn't a guess. One picks up the ability to sense space and direction in the woods after spending countless hours in the same environment playing hide and go seek, searching out hidden patches of wild mulberries, or hiding from, say, a parent. She could venture in any direction and within a mile radius of their home and always find her way back. She was six, and She could navigate.

"We need to sit and wait," her mother demanded.

This made no sense to her. They could find the car in *that* direction, and waiting meant time. Time for her father and siblings to realize they were missing, time for them to make their way back into the woods and find them (if they found them.) Time to grow more hungry and bored. She found a rock opposite from her mother and sat.

"If we go in the wrong direction, we'll get more lost," her mother said, trying to get her to see reason. Her mother talked about the consequences of becoming more lost and described how staying put made it easier to be found—blah, blah, blah. To her, waiting meant giving up, passivity.

"Aren't you glad you brought your winter coat?" Her mother looked at her with a queer smirk.

She knew her mother was hinting at having to use the coat for a blanket in the event of nightfall. A small pit of fear grew in her stomach. There was no way She was going to wait that long.

She did her best to convince her mother where the car was and to trust her directions. It was useless. Her mother didn't budge. An hour passed before She could hear voices. They came from the south, from the direction She had insisted they go. She wanted to say, "I told you so." Maybe She did.

Everyone was quiet during the ride home. Her siblings were mad that the venture took double the amount of time it was supposed to, and yet nobody found a morel. Her father was mad about getting lost. Her mind was troubled too. Resentment took hold of her heart. If her mother had only listened to her, had taken action, they would have made it out of the woods under their own power. Instead, they waited. They waited to be found, like two morel mushrooms sitting on their logs. She resented her mother's lack of faith in both of their abilities. It took her the whole ride home to understand and a lifetime to relearn this choice in life: sit in the woods or take action.

THE SALAD BOWL

Her mother spent time in and out of psychiatric hospitals. It wasn't unusual for her to come home and be told, "By the way, Mom's in (insert hospital here)." And She'd deflate, because She'd thought the last hospital stay *was* the last hospital stay.

Her mother would be gone for weeks at a time, and She never knew when her mother would return. It wasn't like a vacation with a departure and an arrival. However, every time her mother left, her mother returned. Sometimes her mother had gotten a haircut while away or appeared fuller in the cheeks, and She thought maybe her mother had been on a vacation. On one return in particular, the woman standing before her was not the woman who had disappeared weeks before. Her mother was busy and focused.

This time, She lay on her parents' bed and watched

her mother unpack a green suitcase and tell stories about people met along the way—in the hospital, or was it on vacation?

"I made some new friends while I was gone," her mother said while unpacking. Her mother came across articles wrapped in paper towels. Souvenirs from her trip?

She watched as her mother treated these items like the advent wreath at Christmas. A particularly large item was retrieved from between a nightgown and a tattered pair of underwear, and after the pedals of bleached paper were peeled away, a shinny wooden salad bowl sat on the center of the queen bed. Arts and crafts seemed to be a big hit and a treatment for mental illness. She watched as her mother pulled sweatpants and booties out from the suitcase. Next came a clump of white cotton, and when her mother smoothed the fabric out, She looked upon dozens of crocheted doilies. They were made in art class next to Mrs. So-and-So, who wasn't doing so well.

When company visited and admired the salad bowl, it was never mentioned how or where the salad bowl was acquired. Her mother's departures and returns were unmentioned. Always.

TOUCHING THE AFRO

Different was different, and that was good. Every year, her schoolroom was filled with the same children. Some She'd spent the summer with; others lived out of town, and when the new school year started, they'd be reunited, wearing crisp new outfits and looking a little older—but still the same. They were also the same in one inescapable way: they were all white. Their hair and eye colors varied, but they were white.

The week before fourth grade was to start, the class list was posted on the front doors of the school. It was an exciting time to learn who was to be your teacher and who you could sit next to. Along with Teri and Kathy, She made the three block trek to Central Grade School to look at the list of students and teachers. She pointed at the columns, and her finger traced over the names one by one until She found hers. It was under Mrs. Black's name.

Teri and Kathy were assigned to Mr. Neigert's class. So She would be separated from them. She wouldn't be able to pass notes with them or share jokes or funny faces. She'd be able to see her mates at recess only. Bummer.

The other thing was Mrs. Black was infamous for smelling like smoke, and there was a rumor that she hid booze in the right-hand drawer of her wooden desk.

On the first day of school, She'd found her classroom and said hello to the well-known faces that milled about. Kelli had spent the summer in Florida and was telling stories of lizards and finding dead jellyfish on the beach. Jesse described chicken pox and how she'd spent two days in the hospital with a fever.

The classroom was set up with kidney-shaped tables instead of the usual individual desks. There were four kids to a table, and there was no seating assignment yet, so She found a spot in the corner and waited for the bell to ring. James, a dirty boy who lived two blocks away from her, pulled out a chair at her table. The furthest chair from her. She took it as a gesture that he was not interested in sitting next to her but would tolerate sitting around her. The class was full of little bodies and jibber jabber.

Then She noticed a girl enter the room. She first noticed the girl's brilliant white dress with ruffled sleeves and an empire waist. The girl looked like a character from

Little House on the Prairie. What was more shocking was the girl was the color of milk chocolate and had hair as dark as the tar they used to cover the parking lot at the Holiday Inn. She'd never seen this girl before and immediately fell in love with her.

The girl looked around the room and saw the empty seat next to her. After some eye darting and uncertainty, the girl made her way over to the desk and sat right next to her. At first, She kept her eyes on the new bookbinder that lay on the desk, but after a minute, She let her eyes wander over to the peculiar person next to her. The girl was scooping items out of a cloth bag—a pencil, a new notebook, and bookbinder like hers. She watched the girl's arm move to and fro, her skin so enchanting and smooth. She noticed the girl's hands next—long, slender fingers, and the nails so pink and such a contrast from the dark base that they appeared to glow.

The girl must have known She was staring, because the stare was reciprocated. She looked away. She'd never been so close to a person of such color. She could hear her mother's voice in her head: "Stop staring; it's rude." This was a quandary. Staring was neither controllable nor avoidable, so how could it be rude?

She peered back in the direction of the girl and the girl continued to stare at her. "Hi," She finally said.

"Hi," the girl said back. "My name is Amy."

That was all it took. She and Amy were inseparable for the rest of the year. She learned that Amy was an Ottawa Indian and that her family had just moved from the reservation into town. It didn't take very long for Amy and her to have sleepovers. She liked going to Amy's house because her mother made fried bread and they'd eat a basket of it while lying on the living room floor, watching *The Dukes of Hazard*. They stayed up all night playing board games and charades.

Once in a while, her sleepover ended on a Sunday morning, and She'd attend church at Peshawbestown, in Kateri Parish, which was where other Indian families went to church. She was thrilled to go, because the church was tiny and quiet, and She was the only white girl.

One morning, when Amy had spent the night at her house, they walked down to their school to play on the playground. To have the entire playground to themselves, swing on any and every swing, to not wait for a turn on the monkey bars was freedom! It didn't take too long for other children to show up at the playground. She thought some of the kids looked familiar, but She wasn't too sure. The other children took an interest in Amy. Not a kind interest. They began calling her names like *dirty* and *ugly*.

She and Amy took refuge behind a mound of dirt,

ready to defend themselves from the name calling. It may have been She or another kid from the other side who picked up the first rock. One after the other, tiny bombs flew through the air. They landed with resounding thuds. She looked at Amy and saw a look of terror on her face. Amy grabbed a rock and flung it into the air, but the rock landed three feet too short.

Just then, She heard a loud howl come from beside her. Amy had been hit by one of the rocks. Her hands dug into the depths of her thick hair, covering the gaping cut left from the sharp stone. Then the blood started to stream down Amy's face.

She stood up and yelled every unspeakable word She knew at their attackers. She called them jerks, idiots, and the unspeakable—motherfuckers. She helped Amy up and grabbed her friend's head, placing her hands on top of Amy's hands. Vanilla on top of milk chocolate, with ribbons of red velvet. They walked their way past the kids. She continued her verbal lashing, promising to find parents and get them all in trouble. The kids just laughed and clapped their hands over their mouths as they screamed, imitating the Indians they'd seen in movies and on TV.

Amy was crying and needed help. Worried, She decided to sprint home to get help from her mother.

By the time She landed on the porch She was so out of breath She couldn't speak. "Blood . . . Amy . . . hurt," was all She could say. Her mother met Amy a block away and placed paper towels on her head and calmed and soothed her until Amy's mother came to pick her up. The look on Amy's mother's face was of disappointment and shock, a look She could never get out of her mind.

That was the last time Amy spent the night.

* * *

It wasn't too long after her new friendship with Amy that her brother brought over a new friend, a black kid from the neighborhood. For that matter, the only black kid in the tri-county area. She was nine and had never seen a real live black person. Never. She'd only seen them on television and She hadn't even seen many of them there. And he was there, sitting in their living room. She was awestruck. She literally could not stop staring at him. Again, rude, but couldn't be helped. She did the same thing with this boy that She'd done with Amy—looked at his hands and his teeth, because the teeth were so white. She never knew teeth could be so white.

"This is Mike," her brother said.

All She could manage was, "Hi."

When the boy's attention was directed elsewhere, She had full freedom to stare at this amazing black boy named Mike. She then realized what She couldn't stop looking at. Mike's hair—a perfectly round Afro. It looked like a sponge growing out of the top of his head—but bristly and course. She jumped on the couch where the two sat. She had to get closer. The two boys were looking at *Mad* magazines, laughing and not paying much attention to her. She couldn't stop herself. If She just reached out, She could touch his hair, feel the texture of something that was so foreign to her. She lifted her arm and spread her fingers out in anticipation of patting what looked like steel wool.

"Whatcha doing?" Mike asked, jerking his head to the right, just as her hand was descending.

She quickly pulled her hand back, embarrassed that She'd been caught.

"You're not touching my hair," he said.

Both boys laughed. Her brother told her to get lost. And that was that. Her one and only chance to touch an Afro had come and gone.

THE DOGS: PART I

Dogs teach children responsibility and patience—sometimes. She had heard through sibling lore of a dog the family owned prior to her arrival in the world. Rufus was his name. It was a funny name to her. Why did they call him Rufus? Was he found on the roof? She would ask her brothers and sister to tell stories about Rufus and what life was like with a dog.

She was denied the experience of a dog due to her brother's allergies to fur and trees. They found out about his tree allergy the morning after their father lugged a Douglas fir into the den. The Christmas tree had thawed overnight and emitted sap or pollen, which attacked her brother's eyes. He emerged from his bedroom the following morning with a wet compress over his eyes and nose. Her brother announced he'd sneezed a total of two hundred times that night. He said there were actually more but that he'd lost count. When her brother removed the cold compress and revealed his eyes, they looked like two pools of milky tomato soup. What was most starting was the iris of each eye was a deep mossy-green. Somehow the color of his eyes had changed overnight from brown to green. This shocked everyone. Her mother fretted over the boy, trying to figure out if they should take a trip to the doctor for a shot or a pill.

The tree allergy She believed. She didn't believe the dog allergy and would frequently beg her mother to get rid of her brother so they could have a dog. To quell her whining and crying for a pet, her mother bought her a fish. She would stare at the fish and overfeed the poor bastard until the water turned murky. The fish, however, could not run and play with her, nor could it lick her face or fetch. Because She was so lonesome for a companion, She decided to put the fish in her pocket and take it for a walk around the house. She showed the fish her room and the backyard and the patch of wintergreen that grew next to the house.

When they got back to the kitchen after the tour, She reached into her pocket and placed the fish into the bowl. The fish twitched and had a hard time swimming. She decided the fish was tired, so She skipped along to watch television. Later that night, She learned the fish had gone to heaven. Poor bastard.

A few years after the fish died, somehow, by a miracle, their father brought home a Labrador-Irish Setter mixed puppy. They named him Murphy. As She expected, her brother's face didn't puff up, nor did he sneeze two hundred times. The only reaction her brother had was a fit of giggles when Murphy sniffed his crotch.

She and her siblings promised to walk and feed and love the dog, and those promises, heartfelt and true, lasted a month. Murphy grew into a hole-digging, table-jumping, panty hose–eating, barfing-in-your-bed monster. He also, apparently, felt he was a prisoner in the house. He tried to run free at every opportunity.

Her father told a riotous story of taking Murphy out to the woods to hunt, when truly, he was going to shoot the dog. Her father's best friend, Paul Socha, talked him out of euthanasia. When her father got back to the house from "hunting," Murphy (always astute) saw the opportunity to run when the car door opened. On that frozen January evening, her father chased Murphy for an hour around the neighborhood, into back alleys and quiet roads. He prayed the dog would get hit by a car and end his misery.

Eventually, her father's frozen hand clamped onto the soft skin and fur around Murphy's collar. His rage at its height and his patience in the gutter, he leapt up and punched the dog square on the head. Murphy went limp as a rag, the dog's pink tongue spilling over his teeth and onto the icy ground. Her father thought he killed the dog and put its body in the trash can, next to the garage. Where else would one put a dead dog when one wanted the dog dead?

An hour later, the phone rang. It was the next-door neighbor, Mr. Bash, who was the quintessence of a crappy neighbor. He would yell at anyone for stepping on his grass, and he didn't talk, he grunted or swore. She learned most of her swear words from Mr. Bash, as he yelled at his own dog on a daily basis. For the longest time, She thought Mr. Bash's dog's name was Little Bastard. One couldn't hate Mr. Bash too much, because of his eyes. He had eyes that diverted in unnatural directions and glasses so thick that his eyeballs looked minute and fragile.

Mr. Bash was on the phone, screaming that Murphy was—at that very minute—digging holes in his front yard.

THE BRAT: PART II

Being the fifth and the youngest child in her family posed more challenges than rewards. The ability to be heard over the deafening storm of chaos and seniority of her siblings was as elusive as privacy.

Once, She got up in the middle of the night to vomit. This included a long trek down a dark, bare hallway to the back bathroom. She hated to vomit. Not that anyone likes to get sick, but the experience left her shaking and crying every time. Maybe it was having her airway cut off or the feeling of being out of control that made her weep. This early morning, She leaned over the toilet and prayed She'd feel better when it was over. She flushed and looked over her shoulder. Her sister, in her light blue nightgown was standing by the shower, watching. How long her sister had been there, She didn't know.

"Are you done?"

"I just got sick," She said through quiet sobs.

"Feel better?"

She nodded and wiped tears from her cheeks. Her sister motioned for her to go back to bed. She thought it odd that someone would want to watch another person throw up. It was painful enough to go through. Why would anyone watch such a gruesome event? She figured out two things that night. She realized her sister was one tough chic and would be *the* one She'd go to if She needed help. She also came to understand that privacy was a commodity.

The second event of bratty behavior happened one day in the living room. Her brother, the one who tormented her the most, the one who physically marred her legs with bruises and teased her with name calling, wanted to roughhouse. She played along. It started with Indian leg wrestling and led to noogies and intentional tripping. Her brother ended up on the floor, laughing at her inability to physically take him down. She saw his head rolling back and forth as his giggles filled the room. With each turn of his head, his little pink ears appeared like spring flowers in the middle of a field. A thought flashed in her mind, and She ignored the possibility of any consequences She may face. She wanted to inflict pain. Her hand took the form of a cup, and She swung her arm up and around and down with the full force and speed of a comet returning to earth. Its journey ended with a sharp popping sound.

She watched as her brother writhed and screeched in pain. The cupped hand sent such a wave of agony through his ear that he could do nothing but cry. She didn't know where She'd learned such an awful trick, but She regretted the act as soon as She pulled away.

His cries brought their mother into the room. And for once—or twice—her mother didn't take her side. She was sent to her bedroom for the afternoon. While sprawled out on her bed, a foreign feeling suddenly came over her. She had, for the first time, brought her brother down. It was a victory She'd only dreamed about. Instead of her being on the floor squealing and twisting, it was him. Ha! But She had the feeling of victory before, as She often got her way. That day the feeling, so strange and unsettling, emerged in her stomach and fanned out into her frame and pulsed in her brain. It was the feeling of utter empathy and sorrow for her brother's pain.

CONFRATERNITY

It was the beginning of a long, spiritual battle. Her mother insisted She attend confraternity of Christian doctrine. What others dubbed CCD, She described as "living hell." Like her brothers and sister before her, every Monday evening, She walked to St. Francis School to attend one hour of Jesus school. Some days, if She stole a few quarters from her mother's purse, She could stop at Deering's Meat Market and buy a pocketful of Squirrel Nut Zipper candies, peanut butter cups, and various mints. In many situations, She had learned to pacify herself with candy, and this one was no exception.

Once in the schoolyard, She was ignored by a familiar mix of kids—kids She'd seen in the pews at Sunday Mass or after mass, when everyone gathered for donuts and coffee. The kids were shuttled in from other schools, or they walked from various neighborhoods. They were like convicts sentenced to one evening a week in jail. These kids didn't go to her school. They weren't her friends. Her friends were out riding bikes and playing games in the street like Ghost In the Graveyard and Hide and Go Seek. Her friend's parents didn't care about spiritual health or punishment. They were free from God in the structured and forced way. She was often chided and mocked for having to sit and learn about the Father, the Son, and the Holy Ghost. Her friends would crack jokes about classes. "What did God say today?" they would call out. Or, "Too bad you have to leave. Say hi to Jesus."

It was around Christmastime, and all the children's coats and boots were piled in the corner of the classroom. The smell of sweat and feet fumed from the mound of wool and goose down. All the other children had their best attitudes on because Santa, not Jesus, was watching. She learned about the birth of Jesus years before and thought it was a boring story. So a baby was born and some people showed up with gifts. What was the big deal? The other children swam in the delight of the season, while She sat at her desk fuming with resentment and rage. She was done.

That very night, She was supposed to be enjoying a sleepover at Kerry's house. They were supposed to play records and talk about boys and stay up late. They were supposed to have *different* girls spend the night too, (you know, girls who didn't hang out all the time, whose parents were involved and mandated after school activities). All the girls were to play practical jokes on each other like squirting body lotion inside an unattended sleeping bag or dousing someone's hair with shaving cream. Good fun. And not only was She going to miss out on it, but sure as Jesus was crucified, She would be pooh-poohed for her absence and left out of any historical reference to the evening's events.

The CCD assignment that Monday evening was to draw a picture of what She would give to Jesus for Christmas. A blank piece of paper lay on the desk in front of her. The others drew with vim, and She sat staring at the page before her. She contemplated the vision in her head for a moment. Should She draw it? She'd drawn it a number of times before, usually in notes passed back and forth between her friends. She decided it would be the best way to get back at Jesus for his role in her current circumstance. The image was unmistakable—squiggly lines of odor coming off a mound of stacked logs. Pulling her hand and pencil away from the paper, She gazed upon her drawing. The perfect pile of feces. The joy it gave her to give back the pain that had been inflicted upon her! Her anger lifted as She passed the drawing to the person

41

in front of her, as all pictures were collected by the teacher.

One by one, the teacher grabbed pictures from the pile of submissions and held each drawing up to the class for the fellow prison mates to see. She asked each artist what his or her drawing was and what it represented to Jesus.

She saw a pony and a heart, and someone had drawn an impressive rainbow. Her picture was coming up, and the excitement and anxiety build up in her chest. The teacher flipped over the next drawing and her eyebrows knit and a look of confusion crossed the teacher's face. She knew what the teacher was looking at. A big pile of shit. Not surprisingly, She wasn't asked to describe her drawing or what it represented to Jesus. But She had a good story to tell the next time She saw her friends.

BETTER CHEDDAR

Terri was her best friend. The kind of friend who will hold your hand if you're sobbing from a fight with a sibling or parent. The kind of friend who may spend a rainy afternoon with you and sit for hours staring at an album cover depicting Armageddon and help contemplate the end of the world. Just saying, Terri was that kind of friend.

They shared an alleyway. Terri lived on Eighth Street, She on Seventh. They met for the first time in second grade while walking the four blocks to school. From that day on, and for years to follow, She would wait for Terri to emerge from around the neighbor's garage. Usually, Terri ate her breakfast on the walk to school. Terri liked bagels, pop tarts, and macaroni and cheese.

During the summer they were inseparable. One of their favorite pastimes was to walk to Clinch Park and spend the afternoon digging holes in the sand and splashing in the water. A lunch was packed, usually with two bologna and cheese sandwiches with extra Miracle Whip and four cookies to share. Being the thief, She would lift some loose change out of her mother's purse to buy a blueberry Slush Puppie.

On one particular day, Terri laid her towel across the hot sand and took off her shorts and T-shirt. At this point, She still wore a one-piece bathing suit with much modesty. But Terri had a body to support a bikini. They dug through their backpacks to find baby oil, pieces of sticky candy, and a lunch box thermos that contained cold grape Kool-Aid.

The pair lay in the sand and made plans for the future.

"I'm going have my own apartment and adopt ten kittens," She said.

"Ten calico kittens, like the one we saw last week," said Terri.

"Awweeeee," both girls cooed.

Terri said, "We should get a place together."

"Okay. And we can have parties and friends over all the time. And I won't have to go to church."

"Don't forget, no bedtime. We'll be much cooler than our parents," Terri said.

When their skin became too hot, they sauntered into the water and played games and did underwater hand stands until both were too winded to continue.

When lunchtime came, they found the picnic table next to the lifeguard stand. The brown paper sack that contained their sandwiches had been in the sun for a few hours. It didn't matter that the white bread had become hot and soggy, the bologna slick with Miracle Whip oil, and the cheese curled at the edges. They ate happily.

Terri reached into her backpack and produced a box of Better Cheddar crackers and a can of Coke. "This is my new favorite food," Terri said. "I want it at my wedding. I could eat it for breakfast." Terri popped an orange disk into her mouth and rolled her eyes as if in ecstasy.

"It's a cracker."

"No, it's the best, yummiest food. Don't try one; you'll want more." Terri shook the box of Better Cheddar crackers.

She was being taunted. She reached for the box.

Terri snatched it away. "I need to eat a few more before I can share." Terri laughed and began stuffing the crackers into her mouth. Yes, stuffing, because it wasn't one cracker at a time but handfuls.

"They're so good!" Terri mumbled through a mouthful of what was now a pasty ball of orange dough.

Terri washed the glob of cracker down with a swig of Coke.

Watching intently, She held her breath. She knew what was going to happen next. It happened every time Terri drank a Coke. Terri belched, and not in a dainty, girly way, but in a guttural, nasty way.

She couldn't help herself and began to giggle. Burping made her giggle every time because She, herself, couldn't burp. Some genetic deformity in her throat kept her from burping, unless She was going to throw up.

True to form, Terri puffed up her chest and opened her mouth like she was going to scream. There it came, a blast of stomach air that made a sound like a male walrus at the peak of spring mating. She stared at Terri and laughed, as She always did. But something happened that She didn't expect. Terri burped too hard, and She saw an orange tube of semi-digested Better Cheddar pop up in the back of Terri's throat. She thought Terri looked like a wicked Pezz dispenser. The sight of this sent her into a fit of laughter. Tears rolled down her cheeks and She felt it was okay . . . okay that She couldn't breath for if She died in that moment, it would be all right. For several minutes, She couldn't speak. As soon as She regained some composure, her mind would replay the image of the orange dough resurrecting in the back of Terri's mouth and She would be lost in tears . . . again.

"I tasted that," was all Terri had to say, and again She was gone, freed, lost.

POT

She was ten when She met Kerri. It was an innocuous meeting on the playground that gave no hint of future events in their friendship. Kerri, who lived a few blocks away, invited her over after school. Kerri lived with her mother and cats in a little two-story bungalow. The porch was painted gray, and the rest of the house was the color of scrambled eggs.

When She entered Kerri's living room for the first time, She saw dozens of Barbie and Ken dolls scattered over the living room floor. It looked like a mass murder crime scene. Dismembered arms and legs and torsos were tossed around, and one of Barbie's bodies had Ken's head on its shoulders—a modern-day Franken-Ken. She never liked playing with Barbie dolls and feared the next few hours were going to be torture. She was wrong. Instead of engaging with the Barbie's, Kerri brought out her two cats, and the girls tied string and ribbon to their tails and dressed them up like babies. That lasted as long as the cat's willingness did, and soon they were searching for something else to do.

"You wanna see something?" Kerri asked in a tone that suggested danger or secrecy.

"Yeah!" She said enthusiastically, wanting to impress her new friend.

The "something" was upstairs in one of the bedrooms. Kerri began to giggle and ascended the stairs. She followed, and at the top of the stairs was a narrow hallway in which were three bedroom doors. All the doors were shut, and the hallway was fairly dark. Kerri walked to the farthest door on the right and stood in front of it. Not wanting to go any farther, She stopped at the top of the stairs and watched Kerri spin on her heels.

"You can't tell anyone what's in this room," Kerri said, and placed her index finger over the middle of her lips, making the universal secret sign.

She stood, frozen, and watched Kerri open the door. Brilliant sunlight poured into the hallway, making it difficult to see what the room contained.

"Come here," Kerri called.

She had a sinking feeling in her gut. It was too early in their friendship for Kerri to be bossing her around, but in Kerri's voice lived the command for obedience. And She obeyed and approached. The blinding sun must have crept behind some clouds, because inside the room, it became easier to see.

The room had bare wooden floors and walls so white they might have been bleached. It smelled like moist, rotten flowers and not a piece of furniture or artwork was present.

"Why are there clotheslines?" She asked. From one end of the room to the other, hung half a dozen lines. From each line hung several brown clusters of plant material.

"This is where they dry the pot," Kerri said.

"What's pot?" She asked, puzzled.

"This is pot." Kerri pointed to the flower buds tied upside down to the clothesline. "You smoke it and get stoned."

She still didn't get it, but She watched Kerri act out what it meant to be stoned. Kerri stumbled and her eyes narrowed, as if she needed a nap. She laughed at Kerri's silliness.

"Hey man, I'm so stoned," said her friend.

She didn't understand the poor attempt to mimic Cheech and Chong and wouldn't understand the reference until years later.

THE BRAT: PART III

It was a warm summer afternoon, and the house was quiet. She enjoyed the house on this particular day because all the windows were open, and the smell of stale smoke was replaced by the scent of dune grass and lilacs. The lace curtains moved in rhythm with the breeze, and birds could be heard out the dining room window, nestled in the evergreen bush.

She and her brother were the only two in the house. Their mother had gone on an errand, grocery shopping or visiting friends. She grabbed a flyswatter and began batting away two flies that hovered over the kitchen table. She listened as the perforated plastic made a whooshing noise as it moved the air. With a loud thwack, She killed the first fly and watched as its hair-like legs twitched and then ceased to move. The second fly proved to be smarter, dodging the swatter and never landing. She eventually nailed the black speck in midair, using the plastic wand like a baseball bat. She looked for the corpse on the floor and the counter but it had disappeared. When She looked at the swatter, the little body was wedged within the mesh. Gross. She had to show this to her brother who was in his bedroom reading *Amityville Horror* for the third time.

She didn't knock before entering his bedroom. "Look what I have."

"Get out of here," he said. It was his customary answer.

She didn't take his dismissive response very well and walked up to him as he sat on the floor. He didn't look up from his book. She wasn't going to show him the fly like originally planned, but in a different way. She stood next to him, and when he sensed her weight shift the floorboards, he half turned over to look at her. She had the swatter in one hand and with her index finger pulled back the panel and flung the little dead fly on her brother's face.

"What the hell!" That's all She heard.

She dropped the swatter on the floor and ran out of the bedroom. As She rounded the plaster railing to the top of the stairs, She saw her brother scramble to his feet and pick up the swatter in his right hand. Panic filled her head as She flew past the first landing. When She reached the first floor, She looked behind in time to see her brother descending, taking three steps at a time. He was gaining on her.

She ran through the dining room, past the kitchen, and into the parent's bedroom. Their bedroom lead into the second living room, from which She made a circle back into the first living room. She thought She could keep this up, running in circles away from her brother. Maybe forever? But he ran track and was much bigger. As She flew through the dining room for the second time, She could feel him right behind her. Though her breath and heartbeat filled her ears, a different sound pierced the air. A sound She knew all too well of plastic moving through air.

Then She heard the thwack as the swatter ripped between her shoulder blades from left to right. The pain was immense. She tumbled onto the floor, rolling around, trying to get away from the sting. The howling must have been heard by the neighbors.

Her brother yelled something at her which included the words *bitch*, *brat*, and another that started with a *b*. She couldn't make sense of what he was saying, nor did She care. He eventually walked away, back to his bedroom and his book.

Later in life, when She'd watched *Platoon* and saw

Willem Dafoe as Elias being gunned down in the jungle and the haunting scene of him with his arms in the air as he took bullets to his back—that's how She remembered her blow and fall to the floor. So dramatic.

She didn't want to get up. With every movement the pain from her wound flamed like her skin was on fire. After a few minutes, She could tough her way through the pain enough to move into the bathroom. She shut the door and sat on the counter with her back to the sink and mirror. She lifted her shirt like a curtain going up to reveal a horror story. She looked behind herself to see the pale skin of her waist and lower back emerge in the mirror. She wasn't prepared for what She saw next. Her skin was a deep purple and red, and the welt that puckered and pulsed was in the perfect shape of a flyswatter.

When their mother got home, She didn't hesitate to lift up her shirt to show the wound. Their mother stood in the middle of the kitchen, grocery bags still in her hands, and gasped at the sight. With one swift movement, the groceries were on the counter and their mother's purse was flung through the air and onto the kitchen table.

"I'll kill him," her mother said, and made a beeline for his bedroom.

The breath She held in her chest quietly escaped her lungs. She crept into the first living room and approached the bottom of the stairs. She could hear their mother's voice, thundering and rough at first, then turning to a shrill pitch as she began delivering slaps to her bother. The sick feeling returned to her as She heard her brother lament and plead for forgiveness. She'd realized her mother, in no uncertain terms, was a loaded gun, and She'd pulled the trigger, aiming a much bigger wrath toward her brother than expected. And for the first time, She hated the brat She'd become.

SMOKING

Sometimes her mother would get mad while smoking. This was amusing. Billows of smoke would come from her mother's nostrils and mouth, as if she were a dragon—an angry, fire-breathing (or at least smoke-breathing) dragon unleashing an unending pith of fury.

Unlike her mother, She hated smoking, the way it smelled, mostly, and filled their house with a perpetual cloud of white. Some days it was so thick and heavy She could raise her arm and swirl the fetid fog, churning it to form swirls and fissures.

One afternoon, after school, She was sitting on a swing and was approached by two of her female classmates.

One of them leaned down and smelled the top of her head. "You smell like a skunk."

That was the beginning of a very long and unproductive argument about her general odor and of her awareness of how her mother's smoking affected her socially. She became more confrontational about smoking. Sometimes She would demand that her mother leave the house, or would cough uncontrollably when a cigarette was lit. Once in a while, She'd bring her hands up to her throat, the universal sign for choking, and roll her eyes into the back of her head in an attempt to communicate disappointment. Her mother chuckled from the gut, amused and unprovoked.

* * *

It was one of those pretty fall days. The sun was very bright, and a light breeze blew the newly fallen leaves across the sidewalk. She was on her way to Teri's house because Teri had called, inviting her to come over and hang out with Kathy and Kerri and her. Teri lived on the bottom floor of a duplex that sat on the corner of a busy road and a cross street. Traffic could be heard from every room at all hours. More annoying was the traffic light a block away from Teri's house. This made semis stop, and their brake lines popped and moaned and shook the windows within their frames. It was a house of unrest.

She knocked at the door and heard movement and some whispering.

"Come in!" Teri called. This made her nervous. She had been caught in ambushes before, and this situation had the makings of another one.

She opened the door and entered. The dining room table was empty, so She looked to the right, into the living room. Empty. She heard giggling coming from the kitchen area and wandered toward the open door. Nobody was in the kitchen either. Just beyond the kitchen was another room, maybe a mud room at one point or another. It didn't hold much but a chest freezer and some dirty blankets. She knew her friends were in this room. Smoke seeped and flowed from the top of doorframe. Her eyes grew wider and wider as She inched her way in.

"What the . . . ?"

All three friends faced each other, each with a cigarette in hand.

Kerri was the first to speak. "You want one." Kerri produced a pack of Salem menthol cigarettes from a coat pocket, the same brand Teri's mother smoked. All She could do was stare with her mouth open.

"Come on. We're all doing it," Teri said in a snide tone of voice.

"You know you want to," said Kathy.

She waved her hand in front of her face and coughed a little. "Gross."

"You're gonna smoke with us," Kerri said.

This sent a small wave of panic through her. "I'm never going to smoke." She stood her ground and grabbed the pack of Salems out of Kerri's hand. She pulled one out of the pack and placed it between her index and middle fingers. "Look, I'm so cool." She threw her head back and began to wiggle, hoping the distraction would change the focus away from smoking.

This made Teri and Kathy laugh. But not Kerri. Kerri raised the lit cigarette to her lips and took in an incredibly long drag.

She didn't stop looking at Kerri nor Kerri at her. The plume of smoke that exited her friend's mouth was enormous and enveloped her head. At this point, both Teri and Kathy had extinguished their contraband.

"Why not? Too good to smoke with us?" said Kerri.

Kathy and Teri looked at her with raised eyebrows. This was a clincher. If She said yes or no, She was equally screwed.

"Hey, Kathy, grab her and hold her down," said Kerri.

All three of them had a look of surprise and excitement, like what Kerri said was a good idea. Kathy easily outweighed her by sixty pounds, and though slow and lumbering, could pin her.

She spun away from her friends and ran toward the dining room door, but She felt Teri catching up. She would never be able to open the front door in time, so She darted into the living room, which was too wide open to do her any good. There was no hiding or locking herself away there. Kathy came around the corner, body undulating with rolls of fat, feathered hair parted in the middle of her head.

She ducked and pivoted easily past Kathy and back toward Teri, who continued to guard the door. She had no choice but to go into the kitchen again. Kerri waited with a lit cigarette.

Upon entering the kitchen, She slowed down and went toward the refrigerator. Kathy used her massive, fleshy arm to hold her against the cool metal doors.

"Easy there, Fats," She said, knowing the statement would burn a little bit.

Kerri slowly walked toward them, holding the cigarette like a candle at midnight mass. Teri was in tow.

"Smoke it!" said Kerri.

"Come on, pussy," Teri said with a sneer. "You're not better than us."

"Smoke, smoke, smoke," the girls chanted.

They were in a frenzy, Kerri beaming, as she was the ring leader one more time, the master puppeteer.

The cigarette was brought up to her mouth but She shook her head back and forth, refusing.

"Grab her head," Kerri demanded of Kathy.

She looked at Kerri whose eyes were afire with pleasure. She saw Kathy's paw-like hand come up to her forehead, and She slapped it away.

"Give me that," She said. She grabbed the lit smoke out of Kerri's pasty hand and brought it to her lips. She made sure to inhale so as not to be called a cheater or a faker, and She blew the smoke into all three of her friends' faces. "Whoopee! Not a big deal." She used this tactic to deflate the momentum of the event.

Her throat burned and mouth watered with a blackened taste. Kathy's arm released her, and She handed the cigarette back to Kerri.

"Congratulations, smoker," Kerri said. The crazed look on her friend's face was replaced with a look of satisfaction, a look of victory.

SPECIAL EVENTS

Special events were always laced with unexpected twists, usually in ways that were both funny and tragic. Her first confession wasn't spared from this curse. She didn't wear a white dress or patent leather shoes like She did for her first communion. Apparently, bearing one's soul to a priest about all the sins in one's life did not deserve the same fanfare in the eyes of the Catholic Church. Her brothers and sister weren't present. They were much older and busier and probably at a football game or taking naps. The only person present was her mother, who wore a camel coat and the eternal sad expression.

Actually, the general public could never pinpoint her mother's facial expressions or mood. Her mother could be sad, angry, or very, very concerned about something outside of the immediate present. It happened often, when a friend spent the night, the friend would ask,

"Why is your mother so mad?"

She'd look to her mother, either sitting at the kitchen table or at the end of the couch. She'd study her mother's face. Knitted brows, deep groove between the eyes, mouth turned down . . . no indication of hostility. She was trained so well—a slight millimeter change in muscle structure, tiny purse of the lips, or squint of the eyes meant the difference between status quo or self-destruction. More often than not, She'd turn to her friend and say, "There's nothing wrong."

The first confession was held in the evening with all the other "eligible" candidates. About fifty or so kids and their parents packed Saint Francis Church. It was going to be confession en masse, so to speak. The priests—three of them—took chancel with their chairs spread apart so no one could overhear the sins of the others.

After a few explanations of logistics, the candidates formed three lines. There was no joking or light conversation in line. Everyone was breaking a sweat, somber looks upon their faces, for every candidate was told to confess all sins and not leave any dirty action or thought out.

As She stood in line, She contemplated. There was one sin She might save for another time. The debate loomed in her thoughts. Should She confess or not confess the "big sin." She didn't want to shock the priest or the Catholic Church. But She wanted forgiveness. Deep down, She feared being cast away. Maybe the church would think She was too much trouble and unworthy of forgiveness. She decided it would be good to ease into the shallow end of the confession pool, to take it slow and hold back her onslaught of sin. She was going to confess the act of swearing and of lying about being sick so She could stay home from school.

It was her turn to go. She ascended the steps and walked toward the priest and stood rigid in front of him. Priests were horribly intimidating, and She didn't like being so close to one. She believed they had special, high frequency sin radar. Like Santa, priests knew if you were good or bad. And She was *bad*.

The priest smiled, baring yellow, crooked teeth. Her hands dripped with sweat, and her heart beat so fast and hard that it was the only sound in her ears. She started with the rehearsed portion of confession, "Bless me, Father, for I have sinned . . ." When She was done with the prayer, the priest asked for her confession. She talked about the swearing and the lies told.

Her momentum seemed to carry her forward. Before She really knew what She was doing, and against her expert logic-based decision not to reveal the "big sin," She blurted it out. "I stole money from my mom's purse." The pressure and tension She held were released, and She was awash in relief. It was true; confession felt good!

At this point, a mini–time warp opened. The priest said, "That's a big sin."

It took a while for her to process this statement for in that moment She was blissfully light and free from guilt. She was floating in the time warp. Then She came to her senses enough to form an acknowledgement of the severity of the sin. But just before She uttered it, the priest snuck in a question.

"Did you give the money back?"

"Yes," She said. But that was the wrong answer to the question. She was only acknowledging the "big sin." She'd never given the money back. Instead, She'd gleefully hopped on her bike and ridden to the nearest candy counter, stolen money in hand, never looking back.

The priest put his hands on top of her head and mumbled some gibberish. It could have been the recipe for chocolate chip cookies for all She cared. She had just lied to a priest! And She didn't stop him from absolving her! The priest excused her, and She turned and headed back to the pew.

She saw something new in her mother's face—an expression of amusement. Probably that her little girl wasn't going to die with sin on her soul. Little did her mother know.

"How'd it go?" said her mother.

"Horrible," She said as She pulled down the kneeler.

Her mother chuckled. "That bad, huh?"

"I have ten Our Fathers and ten Hail Marys to complete." She clasped her hands together and began to pray. At the end of her penance, She made a special plea to God to forgive her for lying in confession.

THE DOGS: PART II

After Murphy, the family took a welcomed respite from dogs. She was relieved. She no longer had to dead bolt her bedroom door, nor did She need to throw all her personal articles in the closet for fear they'd be chewed and swallowed. The phrase, "The dog ate my . . . *whatever*," was not a laughable cliché among family members but an unending chant spoken through clenched teeth and balled fists. The house, never quiet when Murphy had been alive, took on a calmer chaos.

Murphy had cured her of intermittent longings for canine companionship, and her interest turned to kittens. But the idea of a cat, along with normalcy, privacy, and tranquility would never come to fruition.

One day after school, She walked through the front door and threw her backpack on the floor. Typical. She rounded the love seat and stopped. Jingles. She thought

She heard jingles. From around the corner of the ceramic fireplace waddled a yellow-coated dog. Its ears flopped and swayed. The rabies and ID tags jingled and bounced with each step. Her face took on a silent scream of shock.

Her mother rounded the corner next. "Well, what do you think?"

"Is this ours?"

"Yes, I got her at the shelter today."

To get closer, She knelt before the dog, but it was also an act of genuflection. Murphy had commanded so much attention and dominated so much of her personal space that She thought it proper. This dog was different. It was docile and friendly. Apparently a friend had recommended her mother get a dog because it would cheer her up—elevate her mood. A dog would give her mother something to take care of. And so, enter Buffy.

Buffy was a golden American cocker spaniel. The dog was sweet and cute in the face, but her ears were a Petri dish for bacteria and odor so rank that the dog could be smelled before being seen. Despite this, Buffy proved to be her mother's pet, always present when her mother anchored the west end of the couch. The dog's head rested in her mother's lap like a watchful puddle of love that settled into grooves. Buffy was a baby in the fold of a mother's body.

At one phase of her life when She was much younger, She too would take the same position on her mother's lap. Initially, She would splay herself on the worn, faded green carpet of the living room floor. For extra padding, She would drag her comforter from her bed to create a makeshift nest of cotton and batting. The blanket was like a raft floating on swamp water. She'd watch television from this position until She caught the image of her mother, dimly lit by the floor lamp, whose shade was so stained by cigarette smoke that the light glowed a soft, fuzzy yellow. Even then the image broke her heart. Such a lonely image with an attached sad face. She felt compelled to leave her domain and crawl to the couch and curl up next to her mother. She'd lay her head on her mother's lap, her ear resting in the division of pant legs. She would hear her mother's gut gurgle and pop.

Once, twisting her spine, She stared into her mother's face. "You're percolating."

Her mother smiled and told her to shoo.

"Maybe it's from all the coffee you drink."

A rumble of laughter shook the very lap her head rested on until her body pitched and landed with a thud at her mother's feet.

Buffy never said anything like that and there the dog would lay—the silent observer. Sure enough, listening to the same churning and wheezing of innards.

Not long after Buffy was brought home, the dog began to jerk suddenly and pant on the floor. Her mother took the dog to the vet and it was determined that seizures were causing the fits. There wasn't much to do. Medicine was either too expensive or not available. Buffy had to endure the convulsions, which occurred at least once a month. The episodes were so common that when they happened, family members would say things like, "Do not pee on the carpet." Or, "You can do it, Buffy." Poor dog.

In the spring of 1984, She was told about her parents' official divorce. Her mother was the one to move out of the family home and rent a tiny house on the east side of town. Dogs were not allowed, but it didn't matter anyway. Her mother was so distraught over the divorce that most days She'd find the woman incapacitated in the kitchen galley, completely incapable of attending to anything, especially a dog. So Buffy was left at home.

Soon enough, her father's new wife and two children moved in, and they too had a dog. It was a turd-like wiener dog that had a propensity for snoring like a drunkard. The dogs didn't get along, nor did She with her new family for that matter. And one unremarkable day, when She and her new stepsister came home, they found that both dogs were gone. The wiener dog had been given to a family friend, and Buffy—well, She could only assume Buffy was sent to the pound, though her dad never admitted to anything.

Anger and sadness sprouted, and within the deep confines of the house and behind doors left slightly ajar, resentment bloomed. Whispers of fairness and accountability could be heard, but eventually it came to be the general consensus that it was all Buffy's fault. Buffy was the "stupid" dog, the "dumb" dog. If Buffy didn't exist, then the howling wiener dog would still be within the family fold.

She kept silent, enduring the rants and criticism. She had come to understand the importance of getting the lay of the land when the game and the players change.

THE BRAT: THE END

Dark places were always a problem. Their Victorian house had a main staircase that was dark. At the top of the staircase was a large room, which had no purpose other than to house a worn couch and modest nightstand. This large room was also dark and scary. The strangest fixture inside this room was a door, framed in at the far right corner, and this door led out onto the roof. Standing at the bottom of the stairs, one could hear a little whistle as wind was sucked out of this peculiar door. It was speculated that the door was used as a portal through which to sweep dirt or garbage from the second floor into the back yard. Why else would there be a door that led to nowhere? It proved to be an easy escape for her brothers and sister when they wanted to sneak out in the middle of the night. Her siblings would pass through the door onto the black tar roof and shimmy down the drainpipe, not knowing how they'd get back up.

There were two light switches in the dark staircase, one at the top and one at the bottom. They were old-fashioned switches made of two buttons, one above the other. She never mastered the mechanics of the switch. If She were lucky, She could be at the bottom of the staircase and press the top button on the switch plate and the upstairs light would glow. And She would sigh, knowing if a monster was present in the dark, dark room above, She'd likely see it. More times than not, She'd press the top button of the switch plate and only hear a click. Fear filled her head because She'd have to ascend the dark steps, move closer into the dark shadows of the dark, dark room and slap the button at the top landing to get the light to turn on. Way too risky, for surely the monster would get her before She reached the switch. She spent a considerable amount of her time before bedtime standing on the bottom of the stairs, contemplating how She could get her mother off the couch to help turn on the light.

"Go on," he mother would say.

"I'm scared."

"Nothing's up there. Now go."

Whine, whine, moan, moan. The only motivation that got her up the stairs was anger at her mother for laughing at her. Once angry enough, She'd pound the stairs, one at a time, fully believing her fate was to be devoured by the boogie man. Then her mother would be left to mourn her death.

The basement was worse than the second floor. It was a full basement, not a half basement or fruit cellar. Its walls were thick blocks of concrete. The washer and dryer were relegated to the far-off corner. From the ceiling of bare floor boards and beams hung cobwebs and dust. It smelled like wet dirt and mold. The basement stairs had backings until halfway down. At that point the staircase took a sharp right. Another landing. From there on down there were only slats. Of course, She thought monsters would hide under the stairs and grab her ankles, pulling her into a black abyss. She'd usually scream her head off if asked to go into the basement alone. She had to drawn the line somewhere.

Her mother didn't notice, or maybe her mother noticed but got a lot of entertainment out of watching her preteen daughter squirm at such a childish fear. Fear of the dark.

One day, She was asked to retrieve the clean laundry. After minutes of arguing and refusing, her yelling turned into screaming, and her screaming guided her down into the basement. Surely, her anger would alert any monster that She was not to be fucked with. Still screaming and looking over her shoulder at the empty space under the stairs, She grabbed the hamper of clean clothes. She screamed on the way back up and didn't stop until She reached the kitchen.

Her mother stood in the kitchen and watched her drop the clothing onto the floor. The look on her mother's face was so peculiar that She couldn't gauge its meaning. It was sort of a smirk, but it also seemed to ask, "Who are you?"

She continued to heave and wipe the sweat from her forehead. At the same time, She became very aware of her behavior and how ridiculous She looked. She began to laugh. Surprisingly, her mother began to laugh too.

"Feel better?" her mother asked.

All She could do was shake her head as the two giggled.

* * *

It was a strange time. She knew She was a brat and continued to behave accordingly, but her actions didn't bear sweet fruit. They repulsed those around her.

A favorite pastime of her brother's was to chase her down and knock her to the floor. He'd pin her arms under his legs, rendering her helpless. She couldn't even bite him. Usually She'd be tickled until She couldn't breathe or peed her pants a little. He'd take his index fingers and hammer away at her sternum, but sometimes it wasn't a tickle torture. He'd gather thick spit from the back of his mouth and dangle and slurp the saliva above her terrified face. Clearly her brother had attended some conference titled, "How to Gross Out and Torture Your Sister All at Once."

This same brother was forced to babysit her one evening. She didn't let on that, though his company was annoying, She was glad he was there. Instead, She picked at him about having to stay with her. Once their parents were gone, her brother couldn't stand it anymore. They began the chase again, around the familiar circle until he tripped her just inside the formal living room. He rolled her over and pinned her arms under his legs. She was expecting the spit or the tickle torture.

Instead he squared his face to hers and said the most unexpected words. "Why do you have to be such a bitch?"

It was as if all defenses had been knocked out of her, and the underlying shame surfaced. She began to cry.

"I don't know."

"Nobody's going to like you if you continue to be such a brat."

Deep down—past the brat that had taken over

her relationships, past the tantrums and screaming—her biggest fear was to be left behind, to be hated. She had seen only then, under the mean and dark staircases and within the black, senseless second floor room that certainly housed the most dreadful monster, that She herself was the true monster. Ready to grab unsuspecting ankles and pounce on her siblings and parents.

Her crying morphed into sobs. She knew her brother was right. He stood up and held out his hand, a gentle gesture of peace. She extended her hand to accept his and stood. As they walked to the kitchen She looked back at the floor where She'd just been lying. She saw her body still there, face up, her arms covering her eyes, tears streaming down her cheekbones and into her ears.

There the brat would stay. There, never to rise again.

FLOATER

For Teri and her, swimming in the bay became dull. They both grew tired of handstands and trying to decipher what the other said underwater. That sunny afternoon, both lay at the shore's edge like rag dolls who'd run aground. After some consideration of what to do next, Teri suggested walking the quarter mile to the mouth.

Why not? She hadn't been to the mouth since She'd followed her dad there on an afternoon fishing jaunt. What She remembered of the event was that her line got hooked on an underwater log and She snapped her pole in half when She tugged too hard.

Her father had asked, "Geez, what'd ya do that for?" Like She'd meant to.

The bottom of the mouth of the Boardman River was said to be littered with fishhooks, duck crap, and garbage. That was mostly lore. In reality, the mouth of the Boardman was where the river dumped off into West Bay. The river bulged and narrowed throughout the county and made an anticlimactic ending at its West Bar mouth, or what the townies simply called "the mouth." The water itself was relatively clear; however, the riverbed was stained the color of rust, and some rocks took on the shape of an abandoned boot, a tire or a can of peas.

She and Teri gathered their towels and sandals and started to walk. They told each other stories along the way. Teri said that the night before, she'd had to sleep with her bedroom door barricaded. That was because Teri's brother, Jason, was a wild thing with violent tendencies. Jason composed his life of karate chops, body slams, and other threatening actions. Life got interesting for Teri when Jason lit things on fire. His mood could switch from docile to violent as fast as a head turn. Apparently, the night before, Jason was having a fit of rage and tried taking it out on his sister. Though Teri was older and larger than her brother, the amount of bruises and marks left on her body was evidence of battery and Teri's own inability to fight back. Beyond the physical injuries, the psychological distress was enormous. They both agreed that Jason should be smothered in his sleep, leaving Teri as an only child.

With Teri's problems solved, She spoke of the

possibility of having to attend catholic school in the fall. Her mother was dead serious this time. Come fall, She was going to be enrolled in Jesus school, forced to attend junior high with kids rumored to be stuck up and void of the ability to have fun. Worse yet, She'd have to attend church every day. When the thought of Jesus school and uniforms crossed her mind, as it often did that summer, her stomach would sink and her hands would sweat more than usual.

"Why does your mom hate you?" said Teri.

"I don't know." It was an honest reply. She believed her mother hated her, because if She wanted something, her mother gave her the opposite. If She protested against anything, her mother would make sure whatever it was would happen. For example, piano lessons. She wanted drum lessons, her mother piano lessons. When She was ten, her mother hired a piano teacher to come to the house. The piano teacher wore skirts only, and her hair in a bun, which was always covered by a doily. The teacher was mean, stiff, and strict. For months the piano teacher came and left, and She refused to practice.

Once, a recital was to take place, and her mother was determined She was going to play at it, though her skills hadn't grown beyond "Fur Elise," one of Beethoven's simplest pieces. The day of the recital was interesting.

"I'm not going!" She'd screamed from under her bedding.

"I'll drag you to the car myself," her mother said. She also threatened other real trouble, including grounding.

Once in the Jeep, She crouched in the back foot well and cried the entire way to what She was sure was going to be the most embarrassing public show. Her mother didn't back down or respond to protest in any way. The piano teacher's house was in the middle of a dust field. She was convinced only Satan would live in the middle of a field, void of trees or anything green. She'd come to the conclusion that, yes, the piano teacher was Satan—or a close relative. The bun and doily atop her piano teacher's head were only covering the horns.

She performed, and She bombed miserably in front of well-behaved, well-practiced twits and their parents. Her mother tried to console her as She whimpered on the drive home, but She refused to speak.

Both Teri and She agreed that her mother should be smothered too. She would be a motherless child, and both friends could share a jail cell and raise kittens.

When they reached the mouth, there was nobody around. Most noise came from the thumping of overhead traffic. After a lazy, S curve through the downtown area, the Boardman River ended its existence by passing under a bridge and into the bay. The bridge itself was long enough to support the four-lane Grand View Parkway, but it was narrow, approximately thirty feet. Its underbelly smelled. The structure itself seemed to have taken on the odor of rotten fish and garbage. The rusted girders had cried brown tears down the supporting walls. The cement archway that supported dirt and grass had spray paint markings—someone's initials, with the mark of endearment, TLA.

She looked up into the steel supports and saw tufts of straw and grass—a dozen dove's nests neatly tucked into the corners of the metal planks. A few of the dove's peeked over the edges of their homes, looking down with twitching heads. Their coos echoed.

Teri threw her bag and towel on the rocky shore and told her to do the same. She watched as Teri approached the hand railing that kept onlookers and fishermen from toppling into the murky river. Then Teri anchored a foot on the lowest rung of the railing and hoisted her body into the air. Her friend then reached up and grabbed the lip of the girder on either side and monkey-crawled her way to the center of the river. It was a good fifteen feet, Teri's legs swung free, like they'd fly away if not attached to her. She laughed because Teri laughed.

"I can't hold on!" Teri screamed, and she dropped

like a stone into the water.

She could see Teri's body being pushed by the current. When Teri surfaced, her head looked like it was a detached object, like a beach ball, floating away into the bay. The sight was surreal.

"You're a head," She called after her friend.

Teri swam to the left, to the metal retaining wall that jutted out into the bay. This wall, constructed to lessen erosion of the shore, was a perfect anchor to grab onto. If it weren't there, one would be pushed far into the West Bay. Teri grabbed the wall with tiny white hands and pushed herself onto the rusty metal beam.

She waited for her friend to get back to the bridge before attempting the same maneuver.

Teri was breathless and, upon arrival, grinned ear to ear.

She asked questions. "How cold was the water?"

"Frickin' cold."

"Was the current too strong?"

"No."

"Did you feel garbage on the bottom of the river?"

"No, but it's slimy."

She agreed to climb the hand railing, grab the girder like her friend had, and dangle and swing over the center of the river, but only if Teri came with.

With her friend watching, She went first. She could feel the dove crap crunch under the tips of her fingers as She pulled herself along. She looked over her arm at Teri, who ascended the railing and climbed on behind her. On the count of three, they agreed to drop.

They counted to three in unison, but neither one let go, so it became a contest of who could hang the longest and She lost.

The rush of cold river water stung her skin, and She screamed when She surfaced.

"Holy, it's cold!"

"You'll get used to it."

The sensation of floating free in the river without a tube or raft was terrifying. What if She got swept past the break wall? What if She wasn't a strong enough swimmer? She didn't take any chances. She used all of her strength to reach the shore, her arms and legs burned and felt heavy as She caught her breath.

It took several tries before She could trust that She'd reach the retaining wall, that She wasn't going to be flushed out into the bay. Then She allowed her body to relax and float and enjoy.

They repeated the crawl and plunge into the river a dozen times.

Then Teri made a suggestion. "Let's play war!"

"Okay, but whoever wins has to let go, for real."

The art of war included both She and Teri facing each other, positioned over the river, hanging like clothes on a clothesline. When both said go, whoever wrapped her legs around the other's torso first, won.

She won at war; her legs squeezed Teri's rib cage as her friend wiggled to be let free. She could feel her friend's breath on her face, and She was determined that She wouldn't let go until Teri dropped into the waiting water.

"I'm gonna piss my pants!" Teri chirped.

In tandem, they both fell into the water with a large, painful splash. Her lungs deflated more and more as She giggled. The possibility of sucking in water crossed her mind, but it didn't happen. Both surfaced and made it to the metal wall. A little factoid most don't know is the wall is corrugated. It's not flat or smooth which made it easy to grab. When She got her bearings, She looked for Teri who was a distance *up* river. She asked why.

"I have to go to the bathroom." This was not unusual, going pee in the bay. Bathrooms were scarce and a good ten-minute walk away.

"Go for it," She said not giving it a second thought. She hugged the wall with her arms and let her legs dance freely in the current.

"Watch out!"

When She looked, She saw that Teri was frantic with laughter. Hanging onto the wall, She drew her legs in and hugged her body, with the majority of her torso above the water's surface. Just then, out of the periphery of her vision, She saw a brown lump pitching and bobbing. There, floating by her and waving as if to say good-bye, was Teri's poo.

Her face was a masked scream. She looked back to her friend, who had let go of the wall and was angled to smash into her. And Teri did, full force. Her friend's wailing and uncontrolled laughter echoed within the steel and cement bridge. The force was too much, and She was knocked off the wall and back into the current. The turd was being flushed into West Bay and She along with it.

Acknowledgements

An acknowledgment . . . to say, you are a part of this project and this compilation would not have happened without you, goes to Jeff. For you are MY muse. The person that did not say, "No way," "That's dumb," or "I don't get it." Instead you said, "Yes," "I understand," and "It's possible." What else could I ask for or need?

I would like to acknowledge the people who gave me room to be my imperfect self: Donna, Eileen, Michael, my parents, Paul, Teresa, and Timothy.

And lastly, to Kathy, Kerri, and Teri whose names grace this book and who shaped my childhood with laughter, pain, beauty, and honesty.

About the Author

Bridget Callaghan is a writer and clinical social worker. She lives a quiet life in Northern Michigan with her family. Her other works include:

Thornetta: The Musical (co-author)
The Method Writers (co-author)

She is her first compilation of short stories.